The Archers
2003

To Vanessa Whitburn, who let me come and play in Ambridge.

This book is published **to accompany** the BBC Radio 4 serial *The Archers*. The editor of *The Archers* is Vanessa Whitburn.

Published by BBC Worldwide Ltd, Woodlands, 80 Wood Lane, W12 OTT

First published 1999
This new edition published 2002
Copyright © BBC 2002

ISBN: 0563 48861 1

Commissioning Editor: Emma Shackleton
Project Editor: Cath Harries
Design: Sarah Ponder
Production Controller: Belinda Rapley
Text set in Garamond Light
Printed and bound in Great Britain by Martins of Berwick Ltd
Cover printed by Belmont Press

Events in Ambridge are constantly changing, but we have done our best to make *Who's Who in The Archers 2003* accurate at the time of publication.

Official Archers Website: www.bbc.co.uk/radio4/archers
for Archers episodes in Real Audio, including an audio archive of the last seven days. The site also features daily plot synopses, news, information, quizzes and chat.

Archers Addicts, the official *Archers* fan club.
Write to: Archers Addicts, PO Box 1951, Moseley, Birmingham B13 9DD.
Tel: 0121 683 1951/1952. Website:www.archers-addicts.com

THE AUTHOR
In May 2002, Keri Davies celebrated ten years as producer and later senior producer of *The Archers*. Previous jobs include banking, advertising, media training, PR and the Royal Air Force, and he still looks around nervously waiting for someone to shout 'fraud!' He lives in Birmingham with his wife and three sons and can't decide whether he wants to be a drummer or a DJ when he grows up.

❦ WELCOME TO AMBRIDGE ❦

This is the fourth commercial edition of our pocket guide to Ambridge.

It was originally planned as a quick way for new listeners to learn about the characters in the programme and their relationships, which can be as rich and complex as any in real life. But, to our pleasure, many long standing listeners find the book brings a lot of entertainment and information as well.

So if you've ever wondered if Higgs has a Christian name, or want to know how old Phil Archer is (as he'd probably say: 'I'm fine. And less of the old.'), this book is for you.

Vanessa Whitburn
Editor, *The Archers*

Easter Saturday, 2002. 6pm. I was at my parents' house in Wiltshire when my wife interrupted a delightful nap (I had enjoyed a *very* late Friday night) with the news that the Queen Mother had died. Twenty-four hours later, the Sunday night episode of *The Archers* included a new scene in which our character Jennifer Aldridge related her mother's memories of attending the Queen Mum's 100th birthday celebrations. It had been seamlessly attached to the existing recording thanks to the brilliant *Archers* team and the wonders of digital editing. I was still in Wiltshire, and my boss Vanessa Whitburn, who had masterminded the reaction by phone and email, was still with her family in Devon.

It was a measure of the programme in the 21st century; fleet of foot, employing the latest technologies, and still occupying a place at the heart of our national life.

The creator of *The Archers*, Godfrey Baseley,

4

devised the programme as a means of educating farmers in modern production methods when Britain was still subject to food rationing. Five pilot episodes were broadcast on the BBC's Midlands Home Service in Whit Week 1950, but *The Archers'* official birthday was on 1 January 1951, when for the first time the lively 'dum-di-dum' of Arthur Wood's maypole dance *Barwick Green* introduced episode one to a national audience. Episode 13795, broadcast on 1 January 2003 makes this comfortably the world's longest running radio drama.

The Archers lost its original, educational, remit in the early 1970s, but it still prides itself on the quality of its research and its reflection of real rural life. As Editor, Vanessa Whitburn leads an eight-strong production team and nine writers as they plot the twists and turns of the families in Ambridge, looking ahead months or sometimes years in biannual long-term meetings. The detailed planning is done at monthly script meetings about two months ahead of transmission. Each writer produces a week's worth of scripts in a remarkable fourteen days. To retain listeners' attention in the early years, *Archers* writers drew on the tradition of the 'cliffhanger' which was so much part of its predecessor, the thriller serial *Dick Barton, Special Agent!* The modern equivalent is a blend of stories carefully planned and structured to captivate today's sophisticated audience.

Actors receive their scripts a few days before recording, which takes place every four weeks in Studio 3 at BBC Pebble Mill in Birmingham. Twenty-four episodes are recorded in six intensive days, using only two hours of studio time per thirteen minute episode. This schedule means that being an Archers actor is by no means a full time job, even for major characters, so many also have careers in film, theatre, television or other radio drama.

The episodes are transmitted three to six weeks after recording. But listeners are occasionally intrigued to hear topical events reflected in that evening's broadcast, a feat achieved through a flurry of rewriting, re-recording and editing on the day of transmission.

With nearly five million listeners every week in the UK alone, *The Archers* is the most popular non-news programme on BBC Radio 4 (92–95 FM,

198 LW). It can also be heard world-wide via the Archers website:

www.bbc.co.uk/radio4/archers

The website has been a particular baby of mine in recent years. Through it, we have the privilege of direct contact with our listeners. You'd be hard-pressed to find a more witty, erudite and opinion-ated group of people. And although we who work on the programme may think we are the reason for its continued success, the real reason is out there.

Keri Davies
Senior Producer, *The Archers*

Transmission times: 7pm Sunday to Friday, repeated at 2pm the next day (excluding Saturdays). Omnibus edition of the whole week's episodes every Sunday at 10am. The website also holds an archive of episodes from the previous seven days.

John Archer m Phoebe

John Benjamin (Ben) m Simone Delamain
27.5.1898-2.8.1972   1900-1929

Frank   m   Laura Wilson
1.6.1900-   29.8.1911-
30.5.1957   14.2.1985

John (Jack)   m   Margaret (Peggy) Perkins
17.12.1922-   b. 13.11.1922
12.1.1972

m (2) Jack Woolley
b. 19.7.1919

Philip Walter m (1) Grace Fairbrother
b. 23.4.1928   2.4.1929-22.9.1955

m (2) Jill Patterson
b. 3.10.1930

Jennifer   m (1)   Roger Travers-Macy
b. 7.1.1945   b. 9.3.1944
                     div. Feb 1976

Adam
b. 22.6.1967
(by Paddy Redmond)

Deborah m Simon Gerrard
b. 24.12.1970

m (2) Brian Aldridge
b. 20.11.1943

Lilian   m (1)   Lester Nicholson
b. 8.7.1947   7.6.1946- 18.3.1970

m (2) Ralph Bellamy
26.2.1925-18.1.1980

James Rodney Dominic
b. 30.3.1973

Katherine Victoria (Kate) m Lucas Madikane
b. 30.9.1977   b. 1972

Alice Margaret
b. 29.9.1988

Phoebe
b. 28.6.1998
(by Roy Tucker)

Noluthando Grace
b. 19.1.2001

William Forrest m Lisa

Daniel m Doris
15.10.1896 11.7.1890
23.4.1986 27.10.1980

Edward George
(Ted)
10.1.1902-17.1.1920

Thomas William (Tom)
20.10.1910-5.11.1998
m
Prudence Harris (Pru)
27.7.1921-11.11.1998

Christine   m (1) Paul Johnson
b. 21.12.1931   10.1.1931-10.5.1978

— Peter (adopted)
b. 5.9.1965

m (2) George Barford
b. 24.10.1928

THE
ARCHERS
FAMILY TREE

Anthony William
Daniel (Tony)
b. 16.2.1951
m
Pat Lewis
b. 10.1.1952

Shula Mary
b. 8.8.1958
m (1)
Mark Hebden
20.2.1955-
17.2.1994

Kenton Edward
b. 8.8.1958
m
Melanie
Hardiment
b. 12.2.1972

David Thomas
b. 18.9.1959
m
Ruth
Pritchard
b. 16.6.1968

Elizabeth
b. 21.4.1967
m
Nigel
Pargetter
b. 8.6.1959

Meriel
b. 11.5.2001

Daniel Mark
Archer
b. 14.11.1994

m (2) Alistair Lloyd

Lily
Rosalind
b. 12.12.1999

Frederick
Hugo
b. 12.12.1999

John Daniel
31.12.1975-
25.2.1998

Helen
b. 16.4.1979

Thomas
b. 25.2.1981

Philippa
Rose
(Pip)
b. 17.2.1993

Joshua
Matthew
(Josh)
b. 13.9.1997

Benjamin
David
b. 15.3.2002

ALICE ALDRIDGE

Home Farm • Born 29.9.88
(Holly Chapman)

Parents are *soooo* embarrassing when you're fourteen, especially when they can't understand that a girl might be interested in technical things. **Jennifer** and **Brian** were rather nonplussed when their youngest daughter entered the radio-controlled car race at the 2001 village fête. It was notionally in partnership with **Simon Gerrard** (actually her brother-in-law although they are nearly forty years apart in age), but their win was thanks to Alice's skilful driving – and the disqualification of **Eddie Grundy** for cheating. One thing her parents can understand is Alice's love of her pony, Chandler, who takes up a lot of her time when she's not studying as a day girl at a local private school.

BRIAN ALDRIDGE

Home Farm • Born 20.11.43
(Charles Collingwood)

Poor Jennifer. She thought Brian had grown out of his dalliances with **Caroline Pemberton** and Mandy Beesborough, remaining tragically unaware of his latest fling with **Siobhan Hathaway**. Brian tried his best to keep both women happy, blaming his stressed appearance on collapsing world grain prices and a complex organic venture in Hungary, but it had rather more to do with the fact that Siobhan was expecting his child. Brian's life is full of uneasy relationships. He needs rear view mirrors and a knife detector at every board meeting of **Borchester Land**. And his previously fond relationship with **Debbie**, his step-daughter and deputy on the farm, took a knock when she married **Simon Gerrard**. Brian suspects Simon is a two-timer who preys on younger women. Hmm... Pot? Kettle?

JENNIFER ALDRIDGE

(Formerly Travers-Macy, née Archer)
Home Farm • Born 7.1.45
(Angela Piper)

Jennifer, the elder daughter of **Peggy Woolley** and her late husband Jack Archer, caused quite a stir in 1967 when she became an unmarried mother with her first son **Adam** (now **Macy**). She later married Roger Travers-Macy, who adopted Adam and they had a daughter **Debbie** (now **Gerrard**), but the marriage didn't last. Jennifer wed **Brian** in 1976, producing **Alice** and the older **Kate**, who by the age of 20 was taking after her mother, with two children by two different fathers. Jennifer has been a teacher, journalist and published author and still does the occasional local history project. But much of her time is spent cooking, shopping and sharing in the care of granddaughter **Phoebe**. She loves all three activities, but it's best not to ask her to put them in order of preference.

PHOEBE ALDRIDGE

Nightingale Farm Flat • Born 28.6.98

Product of a short-lived relationship between **Roy Tucker** and **Kate Madikane** (née Aldridge), this little mite was born in a tepee at the Glastonbury Festival, prevented from leaving the country by a court order, subjected to DNA testing and named in a New Age ceremony on Lakey Hill. Roy bravely cared for Phoebe following Kate's departure to Africa. But when Kate had eventually 'found herself' – and a husband, **Lucas** – she swanned back expecting to collect the child like a piece of left luggage. Largely thanks to wise Lucas, Kate eventually accepted that Phoebe's home was with her father now. But she still plays the mother card on her occasional visits to **Ambridge**, which can only confuse Phoebe, who sees Roy's wife **Hayley** as her mother, and Kate as a rather exotic Aunty figure.

'*South Borsetshire. Highly attractive, with archetypal village centre – green, duck-pond etc. Offers a realistic daily commuting proposition to Birmingham, and weekly to London. Local infrastructure includes market town of* **Borchester** *and railhead at* **Hollerton Junction** *(both 6 miles). Integral basic amenities (shop, pub, church, children's playground) are still intact. Although there has been limited infill and ribbon development, this village remains grossly under-utilized housingwise and should be considered a Category A development target. NB: On-site social group AB attractors include health club, swimming pool and golf course, all subsidiary activities of* **Grey Gables** *Hotel – see Annex G on the takeover potential of this asset...*'

Extract from confidential report prepared by Jackal Associates for **Matt Crawford**, Chairman, **Borchester Land**.

Early in 2002, **Lynda** and **Robert Snell** had cause to regret the river frontage which gave their home such an attractive prospect. Swollen by heavy rain, the Am broke its banks and inundated the building. Fortunately the flash flood receded after only a few hours, but it took weeks of work to restore the six-bedroomed Victorian house, and months before the landscaped gardens recovered. The gardens in particular had been the work of years for Lynda, a keen and opinionated gardener, who had established a low allergen area to which she can retreat when struck by her annual affliction – hay fever. Adjoining the Hall is a small paddock which near-neighbours the **Grundys** have tried to appropriate by stealth. A cow, a pony and a rickety JCB have all found their way there – temporarily.

AMBRIDGE ORGANICS

Harcourt Road, Borchester

Pat and **Tony Archer**'s organic shop is managed by their daughter **Helen**. As well as the **silent** Anya, it also employs **Kirsty Miller**, the girlfriend of their son **Tom**. After all, nepotism begins at home.

MARJORIE ANTROBUS

Nightingale Farm • Born 1922
(Margot Boyd)

Marjorie – 'Mrs A', as she's known to many villagers – is of that dying breed of women who never had a paid job and yet worked full time in the service of country and community. In her younger days, it was as wife to 'Teddy', who brought the traditions of British administration to the African continent. After his death, she became the bastion of **Ambridge**'s parish council and the PCC, and occasionally deputized for **Phil Archer** as church organist or panto accompanist. But as she approached her eightieth year, Marjorie started to become more fragile. After many years as a breeder, she had to give up her last remaining dogs, and she became more reliant on **Hayley Tucker**, who lives in the flat upstairs with husband **Roy** and his daughter **Phoebe Aldridge**.

Brookfield Farm • Born 15.3.02

Ben's conception – on a hay cart on a warm June night – was blissfully bucolic. But so soon after breast cancer, the pregnancy posed additional health risks for **Ruth**. Fortunately all was well, and the labour was so quick that **David** had to draw on a lifetime's lambing and calving experience as he became an emergency midwife. **Pip** loved having a new baby to bath and dress, although for a while **Josh** worried that he was going to be replaced. **Ruth** found that as a mother of three she couldn't be as active on the farm as she was used to, which put a lot of pressure on **David**.

Brookfield Farm • Born 18.9.59
(Timothy Bentinck)

Following **Phil**'s much delayed retirement and after a bitter family squabble, David and his wife **Ruth** finally took over the running of **Brookfield Farm** in 2001. They've struggled through some difficult years, facing falling farm incomes, BSE, foot and mouth and worst of all Ruth's breast cancer, but David has plugged away doggedly at every challenge that has come his way. With Phil's help now limited, **Bert Fry** getting on and Ruth busy with their young family, David struggled to keep on top of the relentless round of work at Brookfield, especially marketing quality lamb through The Hassett Hills Meat Company – a 'joint' venture in more ways than one. Contracting out the arable to **Home Farm** seemed like a good idea, although David found relinquishing control no easier than his father had done.

Bridge Farm • Born 16.4.79
(Louiza Patikas)

Pat and **Tony** have had a lot of worries over Helen's relationship with **Greg Turner**. So has Helen, as it took a long time for him to reveal trivial details of his past life. You know; wife, children, vasectomy... Helen's a bit of a dark horse too, although she's also been likened in uncomplimentary ways to other animals, especially female ones. And particularly by **Hayley Tucker**, who, after the death of her boyfriend John (Helen's brother), briefly became almost a surrogate member of the family. Outraged Helen eventually drove the cuckoo from the nest. Determined to draw on her HND in Food Technology and How to Annoy People, Helen bulldozed through a cheesemaking project which saw a lot of expense – and binned cheese – before Bridge Farm Blue went on sale at **Ambridge Organics**, where Helen is manager.

JILL ARCHER

(née Patterson)
Glebe Cottage • Born 3.10.30
(Patricia Greene)

Jill was once an unashamed townie, but through 40-plus years of marriage to **Phil** she grew to be the consummate countrywoman. Never far from the Aga at **Brookfield**, Jill brought up four children – **Kenton, Shula** (now **Hebden Lloyd**), **David** and **Elizabeth** (now **Pargetter**) – and took a full part in village affairs, through the church, WI and parish council. When she and Phil moved to their retirement cottage in 2001, Jill feared that her role at the heart of Brookfield would somehow end. No chance. She continued to run the farm's Bungalow and Rickyard Cottage as holiday lets, and retained her bees and hens in the orchard there. Jill's caring, practical nature is always valued by her family and by other villagers, and with a new grandchild she had plenty to keep her hands full.

Brookfield Farm • Born 13.9.97

When **Ruth** went into labour, keen cricketer **David** was in the middle of the innings of a lifetime, but he was persuaded to leave the field to see his son born. Ruth and David are fortunate in having a childminder/babysitter so close at hand, and when the farm is busy Josh sees as much of his grandmother **Jill** as he does his own parents. Josh was worried when he was replaced as Ruth and David's youngest son by the arrival of **Ben**. But they managed to persuade him that they had no plans to send him back to the shop.

Sponging, er lodging at Lower Loxley • Born 8.8.58
(Richard Attlee)

Aone-time merchant navy officer, **Shula**'s twin often gets out of his depth financially. He's been bailed out more times than a leaky dinghy, usually by **Phil** and **Jill**. Having failed as an antiques dealer, Kenton tried his luck running sailing trips in Australia. He soon needed another handout to pay off a tax debt, confessing that for residence reasons he had married a Sheila called Mel. The marriage of convenience worked for a while, and they even had a daughter, Meriel. But Mel eventually tired of his... well it had two syllables and began with 'B'. She threw him out and he returned to **Ambridge** to raise tempers at Lower Loxley and Brookfield, raise funds for his next dodgy business venture and raise false hopes in the heart of **Kathy Perks**.

(née Hardiment)
Somewhere in Oz • Born 12.2.72

Australian wife of **Kenton Archer**. The family was pleased for Mel and Kenton when they heard in August 2000 that she was pregnant. But given that **Ruth** was undergoing chemotherapy that could have made her infertile, the timing could have been better. The child arrived two weeks late in May 2001 – already taking after her father, **David** quipped – and was named Meriel. But before their daughter's first birthday, Mel had had enough of Kenton's flakiness – and the fact that he owed her money with little sign of paying it back. She showed him the door.

PAT ARCHER

(née Lewis)
Bridge Farm • Born 10.1.52
(Patricia Gallimore)

Meeting Pat was probably the best thing that ever happened to Tony. Not only was she good with cows, having managed a herd of Welsh Blacks in, er, Wales, but she had the entrepreneurial spirit that he lacked. Together, they have built Bridge Farm into a thriving organic enterprise with its own brand yoghurt, ice cream, cheese (thanks to daughter **Helen**) and sausages (son **Tom**). They even have their own shop, **Ambridge Organics** in Borchester. Through all this, Pat has retained most of the radical principles that saw her famously replace Tony's *Daily Express* with *The Guardian* in 1984. **Clarrie Grundy** would certainly say Pat's a sympathetic employer, and she's been a good friend to **Kathy Perks**, even giving her a temporary home after her break-up with **Sid**.

Glebe Cottage • Born 23.4.28
(Norman Painting)

Who are the yeomen, the yeomen of England? Well, one of that breed is undoubtedly Phil Archer, who retired from a lifetime farming at **Brookfield** in 2001. When Phil lost his first wife Grace in a stable fire in 1955, he was too grief-stricken to note that it coincided with the launch of something called ITV. Although devastated at the time, Phil eventually became captivated by travelling sales demonstrator **Jill** Patterson, and they were married in 1957. Despite retirement, Phil still lends **David** and **Ruth** a hand on the farm, but he does have more time to indulge his passion for music; he is the organist at the parish church of **St Stephen's** and his piano playing often accompanies village productions.

PIP ARCHER

Brookfield Farm • Born 17.2.93
(Rosie Davies)

Christened Philippa after **David**'s father **Phil**, and Rose after **Ruth**'s aunt, the eldest **Brookfield** child is universally known as Pip – except when she's in trouble. Pip took well to Loxley Barratt Primary School until brother **Josh** came along, when she started to play up. David eventually solved the jealousy by allowing Pip to show off her brother to her classmates. Fortunately when **Ben** was born Pip was old enough to help out, and enjoyed having a living doll to bathe and dress. When incarcerated at Brookfield during the 2001 foot and mouth outbreak, Pip had some fractious moments. But they were as much to do with her worries about the cows as with the frustration of having to explain modern maths to stand-in teacher **Jill**.

(née Pritchard)
Brookfield Farm • Born 16.6.68
(Felicity Finch)

Ruth has always seen herself as a farmer, not a farmer's wife. She came from Prudoe in Northumberland to work at **Brookfield** as an agricultural student, and married **David** in 1988. The arrival of **Pip** and **Josh** didn't stop her working on the farm, particularly with her much-loved dairy herd, but she had to take much more of a back seat when struck by breast cancer in 2000. A mastectomy and punishing chemotherapy were successful, although the threat of a recurrence hangs constantly over her. Eager to pull her weight after her recovery, she was back in the milking parlour despite an unplanned pregnancy the following year. But when **Ben** arrived, she finally had to slow down a bit. Even Wonder Woman didn't have to save the world *and* cope with three young children.

Bridge Farm • Born 25.2.81
(Tom Graham)

Tom's cooled down a bit since his days as a notorious eco-warrior. In 1999, he was acquitted on a charge of criminal damage, despite admitting attacking a trial crop of genetically modified oil seed rape. This was on land owned by his uncle **Brian Aldridge**, which didn't do a lot for family harmony. Tom works with his father **Tony** on the farm. In particular, he runs the outdoor herd of organic Gloucester Old Spot pigs which his brother John established, and he's had some success expanding that part of the business, particularly **Bridge Farm** sausages. John died on 25 February 1998, which means that Tom's birthdays are inevitably clouded with unhappy memories. Like his father before him, Tom fancies himself as God's gift to women, but most of the time he remains true to his down-to-earth girlfriend **Kirsty Miller**.

Bridge Farm • Born 16.2.51
(Colin Skipp)

Jennifer Aldridge's brother and only son of **Peggy Woolley** and her late husband Jack Archer. For a long time, Tony felt responsible for the loss of his elder son John in a tractor accident, but each anniversary of the death is slightly easier to bear. Tony will never be dubbed Mr Sunshine, but he gets a quiet satisfaction from producing high quality organic milk and veg. Wife **Pat** and her dairy workers turn the milk into Bridge Farm yoghurt and ice cream, and daughter **Helen** converts small amounts into cheese. The veg is sold to a co-op and at the farm shop, **Ambridge Organics**. What does cheer Tony up is roaring round the country lanes in his venerable MG Midget ('mid-life crisis', scoffed son **Tom**), a game of cricket or the excellent products of Shires Brewery.

This large Victorian house with a 17th century core has served as a community centre 'with soundproofed room for rock and roll' and later a field studies centre, but for a long time it remained unoccupied and unloved. The owner **Jack Woolley** eventually decided to lease it to the Landmark Trust. Architect **Lewis** supervised the building's restoration to its Victorian splendour and it is now available to holidaymakers looking for something a little different. As housekeeper, **Freda Fry** cleans the place between lets.

Grey Gables •Born 1951
(Yves Aubert)

As head chef, Jean-Paul is one of the great assets of **Grey Gables** Hotel. But as his friend and manager **Caroline Pemberton** would tell you, he is a bit high maintenance. If Caroline had a pound for every time she's had to talk Jean-Paul down from his high horse, she'd have, ooh, quite a lot of pounds now.

If the phrase 'a friend of Dorothy's' has a certain connotation, then the phrase 'a friend of Eddie's' has a very different one. **Eddie Grundy**'s long time drinking companion, poaching accomplice and procurer of dodgy gear is not known for his liking for show tunes or dedication to Judy Garland. However, Baggy's New Age leanings can be divined when you discover that his children with his girlfriend Sylvia include Aslan, China, Sunshine and Buttercup.

CHRISTINE BARFORD

(Formerly Johnson, née Archer)
The Old Police House •Born 21.12.31
(Lesley Saweard)

Phil **Archer**'s younger sister. Since back trouble ended her days in the saddle, Chris (as she's known in the family) sold her business and house at The Stables to her niece **Shula Hebden Lloyd**. Practical and resilient, Chris worked hard with horses all her life, while for many years struggling with marriage to an airy dreamer, Paul Johnson. After Paul's death, Christine found happiness with the altogether more down-to-earth **George**, and their retirement meant they could spend more time enjoying each other's company. They might even see more of Peter, Christine's adopted son from her first marriage. He lives away from the village, and travels a lot as an administrator with a symphony orchestra, but turned up as the star guest at her 70th birthday party.

GEORGE BARFORD

The Old Police House • Born 24.10.28
(Graham Roberts)

It's odd that George ended up in **Ambridge**'s former police house, because he was a copper for a few years before spending the bulk of his working life as a gamekeeper. A sort of gamekeeper turned gamekeeper, you might say. George has been a great help to his fellow Ambridge keepers, recruiting and training **William Grundy**. And William's boss **Greg Turner** has often benefited from George's wisdom, gained through an early life that was marred by alcoholism and divorce. Like his current wife **Christine**, George is on his second marriage. He has two children, Karen and Terry, from the first one. A straight-talking Yorkshireman, George plays the cornet, works voluntarily both as a tree warden and a flood warden, and makes a popular chairman of the Parish Council.

(formerly Nicholson, née Archer)
Guernsey • Born 8.7.47
(Sunny Ormonde)

Jennifer Aldridge's younger sister and the widow of **Ambridge**'s last real squire figure Ralph Bellamy, who ended his days in Guernsey. After Lilian's son James (born in 1973) moved to London, his mother seems to have found comfort mainly in gin and the company of attractive young men. The collapse of her relationship with a two-timing gold-digging bit-part actor/model called Scott led to her temporary return to Ambridge in 2001 and a bid to regain her youth via cosmetic surgery. Rich, self-centred and impatient with Ambridge's sleepy ways, she has much in common with **Matt Crawford**. Jennifer was annoyed when Lilian got into bed with Matt over **Borchester Land**'s planned housing development. It was a metaphorical bed, but we wouldn't put it past either of them to find a real one some day.

BERROW ESTATE

See BORCHESTER LAND

*'For business or tourism, come to BORCHESTER, the Jewel of the Shire's! Borchester is a traditional Market Town with all the modern amenities. Our excellent Leisure facilities include the well-patronized Theatre Royal, a compact Multiplex Cinema showing Hollywood's latest blockbusting smashes and well-equipped Municipal Leisure Centre featuring modern Gym and Swimming Pool. Shopper's will be delighted with our range of High Street famous names, plus not forgetting independent retailers like **Underwoods** the Traditional Department Store and **Ambridge Organics** for Speciality Food's. And for housing or outings, the picturesque village's of the Am Vale lie close at hand only a stone's throw away.'*

Extract from *BORCHESTER – TOWN OF OPPORTUNITY* issued by Borchester Chamber of Trade and Commerce.

Property company owning the 1020 acre **Berrow Estate**, including business units at Sawyers Farm and one tenanted holding, **Bridge Farm**. **Brian Aldridge** thought he was moving into the big boys' playground when he became a director, but he soon found that big boys play rough games. With world prices so low, the board has been unhappy with its return on capital, and is constantly looking for ways of screwing more money out of its investment. Brian saw his contract to farm the Estate's 'in hand' land go to a more ruthless outside firm, and was unable to prevent plans for an unsympathetic housing development on old **Grange Farm** land. As the Borchester Land chairman **Matt Crawford** makes Machiavelli look like Postman Pat, Brian would be advised to take a food taster to dinner parties.

BRIDGE FARM

STOCK
65 milkers (Friesians) • 30 followers (heifers/calves)
100 outdoor reared pigs

CROPS
115 acres grassland • 22 acres barley
15 acres wheat • 6 acres potatoes • 2 acres carrots
2 acres leeks • 3 acres swedes
2 acres Dutch cabbage • 1 acre Savoy cabbage
4 acres mixed vegetable and salad crops, including
2 polytunnels

LABOUR
Tony Archer • Pat Archer • Tom Archer • Clarrie Grundy,
Colin Kennedy (dairy)

Tenant farmers **Tony** and **Pat Archer** rent 140 acres from the **Berrow Estate**, with an extra 32 acres from other landlords. Bridge Farm converted to organic in 1984. The dairy's yoghurt and ice cream is sold through a wholesaler and to local outlets such as the **Village Shop**, **Grey Gables** and **Underwoods.** But Pat and Tony would first direct you to their own farm shop **Ambridge Organics** in **Borchester**, which also stocks their own sausages and other meat from the herd of Gloucester Old Spots.

BROOKFIELD FARM

STOCK
130 milkers (Friesians) • 70 followers (heifers/calves)
20 beef cattle (Herefords) • 300 ewes
Hens (small scale)

CROPS
258 acres grassland • 115 acres cereals
34 acres oil seed rape • 15 acres potatoes
12 acres beans • 10 acres fodder beet
17 acres forage maize • 8 acres set-aside

LABOUR
David Archer • **Ruth Archer** (mainly dairy)
Phil Archer (relief) • **Jill Archer** (hens, bees, holiday cottages)
Bert Fry (general) • **Chaba Proganyi** (student)
Biff (sheepdog)

Brookfield is a 469-acre mixed farm which incorporates the old holdings of Marney's and Hollowtree. With **Phil**'s retirement in 2001, **David** contracted out the arable work to **Home Farm** so he and **Ruth** could concentrate on their sheep, dairy and David's personal hope for the future – rearing high quality beef for a local market from Hereford cattle.

THE BULL

*'Hosts **Sid** and **Jolene Perks** invite you to The Bull, a real old English free house serving excellent Shires ales. Play traditional darts and dominoes in the public bar, or try the cosy Ploughman's bar. Food always available – enjoy a snack in the bar, or a good value meal in our Family Restaurant. We open at 10am for coffee – read the newspaper over breakfast. First floor function room features line dancing with Jolene (Tuesdays) and The Bull Upstairs (Thursdays to Saturdays) for the younger set, with CD jukebox, occasional bands and DJs. Available for private functions at other times. Outside, car parking, beer garden with Eccles the peacock and boules piste (equipment available behind the bar). Look for the half-timbered building just off the Village Green.'*

(Extract from *A Guide to Ambridge* leaflet (third edition) available at **St Stephen's** church.)

No 1, The Green • Born 22.6.88

Neil and **Susan**'s son and younger brother to **Emma**, Christopher started at **Borchester** Green secondary school in September 1999. Christopher has had the odd episode of juvenile idiocy (haven't we all), but generally gives his parents little trouble. He's a dab hand with radio controlled cars, coming a terrific second to **Alice Aldridge** at the 2001 village fete. And he's followed his father into the bell tower at St Stephen's. He rang his first full peal – of Grandsire Triples, since you ask – at the Jubilee celebrations in 2002.

No 1, The Green • Born 7.8.84
(Felicity Jones)

Neil and **Susan's** bright and sassy daughter is a keen dancer. After unspectacular GCSE results in August 2000, she got a job as an assistant in the Orangery café at **Lower Loxley**, to Susan's unconcealed distress (damn those **Horrobin** genes...) In 2001, Emma foolishly accepted a lift home with **Ed Grundy**, who ran the car into a tree trying to avoid a deer. The resultant broken leg gave her time to think about the future and she returned to work with the intention of taking some catering qualifications and eventually getting a management job. Although she'll always be close to Ed, who risked his life to pull her out of the burning car, she started going out with his steadier brother **William**; yet another thing for the boys to argue about, and a worry for her parents as they saw her approach adult life.

NEIL CARTER

No 1, The Green • Born 25.5.57
(Brian Hewlett)

Neil worked for a few years as a feed rep, but his mild manner was never really suited to the life and in 1998 he returned to his first love – pigs. Susan wasn't impressed, and not just by the words 'first' and 'love'. Neil runs an outdoor herd of Gloucester Old Spots at **Willow Farm**, and works in conjunction with would-be pig baron **Tom Archer**. In 2001, former partner **Mike Tucker** was disappointed when Neil replaced their pick-your-own strawberries with **Betty**'s hens. Landless **Eddie Grundy**'s plans to monopolise Neil's few acres with compost, turkeys and who knows what else were scuppered by **Emma**'s accident. Neil could have knocked seven bells out of **Ed**, but he contented himself with ringing them – as tower captain at St Stephen's.

SUSAN CARTER

(née Horrobin)
No 1, The Green • Born 10.10.63
(Charlotte Martin)

Susan's not had a lot of luck in her attempts to shake off the bad start that comes with being a **Horrobin**. In 1993 she was forced to shelter brother **Clive** when he was on the run, getting three months in prison when he betrayed her. She tried to get husband **Neil** into a white collar job, only to see him return to the land. Daughter **Emma** went to work in a café rather than on to university (so no pressure on **Christopher**, then...) Susan supplemented her job at the **Village Shop** with a receptionist's post at the surgery, only to see it close in 2002. It left her wondering if the Carter family should look elsewhere if they are ever to achieve the success that Susan so desires.

MATT CRAWFORD

Somewhere posh near Borchester and
a nice place in town
(Kim Durham)

Brian Aldridge's chairman in **Borchester Land** is a Del Trotter who really did make a million, but without that character's redeeming social features. Matt doesn't let a little thing like the planning laws get in the way of his business objectives, or the fact that he is married get in the way of his sexual urges (as **Debbie Gerrard** once found out, to her horror). Brian has won some battles, but Matt still managed to get the **Grundys** evicted from **Grange Farm**, and an **Ambridge** housing development pushed through – albeit for a smaller estate than the mini-Milton Keynes he'd originally planned.

Building contractor Paul Blocker is a man who eats not wisely, but too well. He managed to squeeze himself into the cab of his JCB to perform a comically awful 'Disco Diggers' routine with **Eddie Grundy** at the 2001 **Ambridge** fete.

For **Ambridge** residents, Birmingham supplies the real bright lights, but this cathedral city 17 miles east of the village is a good half-way house. Lots of shops, nice places to eat and drink: a nirvana for the credit card generation. In the evenings, Bannisters café bar is where the young and beautiful congregate until sensible people over the age of 30 have going to bed. Then they move on to Angels club for several hours dancing, preening and 'pulling'.

JANET FISHER

The Vicarage, Darrington
(Moir Leslie)

Formerly a nurse, in 1995 Janet became vicar of the combined parishes of Darrington, Penny Hassett, Edgeley and **Ambridge**. Some parishioners – notably **Peggy Woolley** – couldn't countenance a woman priest and left to worship elsewhere, but most accepted Janet with open arms. And therein lay a problem, because one pair of arms belonged to the local doctor **Tim Hathaway**. Janet fought temptation until it was clear that Tim's marriage was on the rocks anyway, and at last they could plan a new life together. But, given the history, they realised that it would have to be well away from the village gossips (yes, you, **Susan Carter**), so Janet looked for a parish elsewhere, planning to leave **Ambridge** early in 2003.

Glebelands

With his wife Pat, one of the earliest residents of Glebelands, a small development of 'executive homes' near the Green. The Fletchers are the kind of people who move to the country for the air, the views and the wildlife and then complain about the smell, the silage clamps and being woken up by cockerels. Along with **Peggy Woolley**, Derek was one of the parishioners who left **St Stephen's** for All Saints, **Borchester** on the appointment of **Janet Fisher**. When **Hayley Tucker** had the temerity to criticise people who object to new housing destroying their rural idyll, **Roy** traced a poison pen letter back to the charming Mr Fletcher.

WAYNE FOLEY

(Ian Brooker)
Radio Borsetshire
Broadcasting throughout the county on 87.3FM

'Tune into the Wayne Foley Afternoon Show. *With news and views from around the county and the tea time guest. And play spot the personality with Wayne's Usual Suspects competition!*

Something to say? Call Brenda* on the phones.

Every weekday, 2 'til 5.

'Life going slowly? Tune to Foley.'

(*That's **Brenda Tucker**. **Mike**'s so proud)

Baggy and Snatch. They go together like 'drunk and disorderly'. And, to **Clarrie**'s alarm and despondency, they often go arm in arm with **Eddie Grundy**.

BERT FRY

Woodbine Cottage • Born 1936
(Eric Allan)

To the casual observer, there's not much to set Bert apart from the general run of agricultural workers. But don't be fooled, because underneath those overalls beats the heart of a poet. Bert is the unofficial bard of Borsetshire who once had his own column in the **Borchester** Echo. Despite reaching retirement age in 2002, Bert kept plugging away at **Brookfield**, where David and Ruth have often been grateful for his understanding way with their children. Bert and **Freda** have one son Trevor and a granddaughter Amy. Whether as cricket umpire or church-warden, Bert approaches all tasks with the same steady, dutiful approach, which can infuriate the more impatient. But my goodness it pays dividends in his garden, as demonstrated by the numerous prizes he's amassed at the annual Flower and Produce show.

Woodbine Cottage

Freda cleans the house and holiday cottages at **Brookfield**, and is the housekeeper at **Arkwright Hall**. She knocks out cheap and cheerful meals aplenty for **The Bull**'s family restaurant, and at home she keeps **Bert**'s body and soul together with large helpings of hearty traditional nosh. At the annual Flower and Produce Show her cakes and preserves are so successful that despairing competitors wonder if she's made a pact with the devil. But it's not these domestic accomplishments that make Freda seem the perfect woman to a certain sort of unreconstructed male. It's that she is never heard to speak.

DEBBIE GERRARD

(née Aldridge)
Woolmarket Flats, Borchester • Born 24.12.70
(Tamsin Greig)

Debbie, the daughter of **Jennifer Aldridge** and her first husband **Roger Travers-Macy**, has important relationships with two men in their fifties. One is her stepfather **Brian**. And unfortunately, he can't stand the other one; her husband **Simon**. As Brian's deputy at **Home Farm**, Debbie does most of the hands-on work, which results in frustration levels from mild to infuriating when he 'interferes'. And there's a lot of frustration in Debbie's life. Low grain prices have made Home Farm much less of the money machine it once was. And the Hassett Hills Meat Company, her joint venture with **Brookfield** and other farms, has struggled to persuade customers that better quality lamb is worth paying a bit more for. When things get too tough, Debbie gallops away her frustrations in the company of another male – her horse Autolycus ('Tolly').

SIMON GERRARD

Woolmarket Flats, Borchester
'Hey, you're as old as the woman you feel'
(Garrick Hagon)

A student of modern British invective could do worse than to sit **Brian Aldridge** down and start him off on the subject of his son-in-law. It looked like Brian's low opinion was justified when in 2000 a student at the University of **Felpersham** claimed that Simon was more lecher than lecturer. But when the girl withdrew her accusations, Simon seized the moment and **Debbie**'s hand in marriage. Despite Debbie's faith in him, Simon certainly seems to like the company of young female students, but he's either clever, careful or (slim possibility) completely faithful, as no further mud has stuck to him. Some find Simon's Canadian charm a little too ingratiating and there's no doubt he likes to be liked. But **Jennifer** could chat to him about books for hours.

SIR SIDNEY & LADY MERCEDES GOODMAN

Agarage mechanic announcing that he's going to give Sir Sidney's Mercedes a good seeing-to might soon expect a visit from a couple of burly men. Because Mercedes is Sir Sidney's Spanish wife, whose decades of sun-worshipping and couture shopping combine to form an appearance reminiscent of a distressed leather settee swathed in an elegant throw. Goodman's Spanish interests date back to the days when he fought with Franco in the civil war, and he still takes a totalitarian approach to running his food-processing empire, which includes canning factories in **Borchester**, Spain and elsewhere.

A working farm (just) until the bankrupt **Grundys** were evicted in April 2000. The bulk of the acreage was absorbed back into the **Berrow Estate** and the farmhouse sold with fifty acres to **Oliver Sterling**, whose plan to run beef cattle ('hobby farming', scoffed **Joe Grundy**) was delayed by the foot and mouth outbreak of 2001.

'Did you see that Grey Gables Hotel on the telly? It looked nice enough, very swish. Lovely outdoors, park and woods and that. Golf course and all, your Frank'd be interested, and a health club. How the other half live, eh? **John Higgs**, *you know him? He was on it and some funny woman,* **Snell**, *don't think I'd want her checking my reservation. And there was this chef,* **Jean-Paul** *something,* **Aubert**, *yeah that's right. Barking mad. Mind you, French you see, what d'you expect?* **Roy Tucker**, *you know,* **Betty**'s *boy, he come out of it very well. No, not the manager that's* **Caroline Pemberton**, *he's an assistant or trainee or something. That* **Jack Woolley** *must have been tearing his hair out, yes he owns it, why they agreed to let the cameras in...'*

Conversation overheard on the Hollerton Circular bus following three 'docububbles' about Grey Gables on cable TV.

ALF GRUNDY

Gloucester • Born 13.11.44

When the Grundys were farmers, they didn't need to buy any black sheep, because they had one of their own, in **Eddie**'s brother Alf. The Grundys adhere more to their own idiosyncratic moral code than the letter (or indeed word, sentence, paragraph or subsection) of the law. But after his release from prison for breaking and entering Alf committed the ultimate offence; he stole from his family. When Joe was 80, Eddie and Clarrie arranged for him to visit Alf as a birthday treat. It was better than Alf coming back to Ambridge.

CLARRIE GRUNDY

(née Larkin)
Keeper's Cottage • Born 12.5.54
(Rosalind Adams)

If life is ever getting you down, think of Clarrie Grundy and things won't seem so bad. Married to **Eddie**, with **Joe** as her father-in-law and younger son **Ed** a constant worry, she slaves all hours at **Bridge Farm** dairy and in **The Bull** to put bread on the table. And then she has to butter it herself, because the Grundy men aren't renowned for their domestic skills. No wonder she dreamed of moving to France, even if the closest she got was a couple of visits to **Ambridge**'s twin town of Meyruelle in the south of France. Clarrie felt that was a bonus, because usually the best she can do is a trip to Skegness to see her sister Rosie Mabbott. When it all gets too much, Clarrie retreats to the perfumed heavings of her favourite reading material – romantic novels.

EDDIE GRUNDY

Keeper's Cottage • Born 15.3.51
(Trevor Harrison)

With his father **Joe**, Eddie used to be the tenant at **Grange Farm**. Eddie once hoped for success as a country and western singer but was advised not to give up the day job. Ironic, as the day job eventually gave up on him, and Eddie entered his fifties bankrupt and farmless. Ironic too that he ended up renting a house (from **Jack Woolley**) that was originally built for a local gamekeeper, as Eddie has been known to supplement the housekeeping with the occasional trout or pheasant from neighbouring farms. Odder still (not Eddie's words) that that his elder son **William** chose to become... a gamekeeper. Rid of the burden of all the farm work, Eddie says that he's got much more time to concentrate on his other enterprises. Or 'scams' as the rest of **Ambridge** call them.

ED GRUNDY

Keeper's Cottage • Born 28.9.84
(Barry Farrimond)

Once he'd left school without taking any exams, Ed was on the summit of a very slippery slope, but he's had two wake-up calls which might have prevented the decline that **Clarrie** fears. A burgeoning joyriding career was halted when he ran his elder brother's car into a tree, seriously injuring **William**'s girlfriend **Emma Carter**. Although Ed bravely pulled Emma from the burning vehicle, it's no wonder the relationship between the brothers is usually sub-zero. And Ed's growing enthusiasm for drug-taking was soured when **Jazzer**, the one-time singer in Ed's band *Dross*, suffered brain damage after taking ketamine. **Eddie** tries to find work for his son, if only to stop him helping out at their old home **Grange Farm** for class enemy **Oliver Sterling**.

JOE GRUNDY

Keeper's Cottage • Born 18.9.21
(Edward Kelsey)

The Grundys had been tenant farmers 'since time immoral', and Joe still feels the burden of being the Grundy who lost **Grange Farm** for future generations. He finds there is little that will console him, except possibly hitching up his pony and trap and going for a pint at **The Bull**. (Joe is a devout Methodist, except for the bit about not drinking alcohol. Or going to chapel.) Joe used to suffer from a complaint known as 'farmers lung', but it's been a lot less troublesome since son **Eddie** hasn't expected him to do any work. So Joe potters around his garden and, thanks to neighbour **Robert Snell**, has become an unlikely 'silver surfer'. Websites devoted to Vera Lynn are his favourite.

WILLIAM GRUNDY

The Dower House • Born 9.2.83
(Philip Molloy)

It looks like brother **Ed** inherited the Grundys' wilder traits, while **Clarrie**'s respectable Larkin genes were passed to **William**. The elder son takes life seriously, to the point of being slightly stolid, but **Emma Carter** found him sufficiently attractive to go out with. William is lucky enough to have **Caroline Pemberton** for a godmother, and lives in some rooms at her house. To his father **Eddie**'s dismay, William works as an under-keeper with **Greg Turner** at the combined **Grey Gables**, **Berrow Estate** and **Home Farm** shoot. Sadly, William has a low opinion of both Eddie and Ed. Ever sadder, it's probably justified.

SHIV GUPTA

Coventry
(Shiv Grewal)

Accountant Shiv is **Usha Gupta**'s elder brother, and can usually be relied upon to appear at Blossom Hill Cottage when Usha needs cheering up. He didn't really approve of her partner Richard Locke, and when Richard left after that unpleasant business with **Shula Hebden Lloyd**, Shiv did his best not to say 'I told you so'. More recently, perhaps in despair of Usha finding a suitable man by her own devices, he tried to pair her up with an ex-partner of his: Ashok, who was conveniently moving to **Felpersham**. But Usha seemed to prefer the barrister Adrian Manderson.

USHA GUPTA

Blossom Hill Cottage • Born 1962
(Souad Faress)

Usha's keen sense of fun is sometimes overwhelmed by the demands of her job as a partner in **Felpersham**-based solicitors Jefferson Crabtree, but she finds time to drag her best friend **Ruth Archer** off salsa dancing occasionally. Usha's parents were unhappy when she moved to the countryside from Wolverhampton, especially when she was the target of a gang of racists, in which **Roy Tucker** was initially involved. It was hard to forgive him for that, but even harder to forgive **Shula Hebden Lloyd** for her part in driving away Usha's lover Richard Locke in 1998. More recently, Usha has been out with a barrister, Adrian Manderson, and Ashok, an accountant friend of her brother **Shiv**. A doctor, a barrister and an accountant... Single Borsetshire vets and dentists are already polishing their dancing shoes.

Felpersham
(Caroline Lennon)

Things certainly haven't worked out the way Siobhan had hoped when she and former husband **Tim** came to **Ambridge** in 1999, he to be the local GP and she to work as a freelance translator. The first cloud on the apparently idyllic horizon was when a much-welcomed pregnancy ended in miscarriage. Then Tim became close to the vicar **Janet Fisher** and as the marriage foundered Siobhan was ripe for an affair. Enter **Brian Aldridge**. But in April 2002 Siobhan found she was pregnant. She was determined to keep the child, while Brian was as determined that he would not leave his wife **Jennifer**. Thanks to Tim's generosity of spirit, while it was impossible to hide Siobhan's condition, they managed to keep the identity of the father a secret known to only a few in Ambridge. But a secret like that is hard to keep...

DR TIM HATHAWAY

London
(Jay Villiers)

Tim joined the army to finish his medical training, and served for six years in the UK and Germany, where he met his former wife **Siobhan**. When he returned to civilian life, he worked as a GP in Islington before buying the practice in **Ambridge** in 1999. But three years later he was selling up after the collapse of his marriage – and leaving an angry village without a resident doctor. The one silver lining, for Tim at least, was falling in love with **Janet Fisher**, although their relationship meant that she too had to look for work elsewhere so they could be together.

Bunty born 20.2.22
(Bunty – Sheila Allen)

Reg and his wife Bunty were happy to see their son Mark follow his father into the solicitor's trade, and very happy with Mark's choice of wife – **Shula** (now **Hebden Lloyd**). But when Mark recruited an Asian woman – **Usha Gupta** – as his business partner, his parents' disapproval was just as clear. Bunty clashed with Shula's current husband **Alistair Lloyd** over **Daniel**'s education, and was disappointed when Shula opted for the local state primary. So when Alistair decided he wanted to adopt Daniel, it took a deal of cupcake diplomacy from fellow grandparents **Jill** and **Phil Archer** before the Hebdens withdrew their objections and accepted the severing of their legal rights over their grandson. But Shula has made sure that their relationship with Daniel is just as close, despite the adoption.

Grey Gables

Whatever his faults, you can't accuse **Grey Gables**' chauffeur and handyman of talking too much. **Jack Woolley** forgives Higgs' occasional indiscretions because of his talent with chrysanthemums, which have carried off many a prize for his proud employer. He's known as 'John' to very few people – in fact even his mother probably calls him Higgs like everyone else.

Although the bus service around **Ambridge** is pretty dire, just six miles west of the village is a railway station, which means it's easier to get to Birmingham or London (via Paddington) than it is to get to some of the surrounding villages. Ah, the wonderful logic of 21st century public transport...

STOCK
600 ewes • 110 hinds, stags, calves

CROPS
956 acres cereals • 136 acres grassland
75 acres oil seed rape • 100 acres sugar beet
80 acres linseed • 75 acres peas
80 acres woodland • 58 acres set-aside, including:
40 acres industrial rape • 10 acres willow (game cover)

OTHER
25 acre riding course • Fishing lake

LABOUR
Brian Aldridge (managing and relief)
Debbie Gerrard (deputy) • **Greg Turner** (gamekeeper)
William Grundy (under keeper)
Andy, Jeff (general workers)
Fly (sheepdog)

With 1585 mainly arable acres, Home Farm is the largest in **Ambridge** and carries out contract farming for **Brookfield** and other local farms. It's a partner with Brookfield and others in the Hassett Hills Meat Company, raising and supplying high quality lamb to butchers and caterers.

Felpersham
(Peter Howell)

The Bishop of **Felpersham** manages to be liberal and compassionate without being wishy-washy or a soft touch. He is a firm supporter of women priests, but is well aware of the extra burdens they have to bear. **Janet Fisher** was hugely grateful for his support as she wrestled with her attraction to **Tim Hathaway**. And as Tim's marriage deteriorated, Cyril helped her find a path by which they could be together while she remained a priest.

Banged up again • Born 9.11.72
(Alex Jones)

Unpleasant Clive was responsible for turning his sister **Susan Carter** into **Ambridge**'s – and for a while Britain's – most controversial jailbird. After an armed robbery at the **Village Shop**, he coughed to the cops that Susan had harboured him, while forgetting to mention that he had forced her do it. Clive bears a grudge against ex-policeman **George Barford**, who suspected correctly that Clive was behind a series of burglaries in Ambridge after he had emerged from his prison sentence for the Village Shop job. Clive was soon on his way back inside.

THE HORROBINS

No. 6, The Green, and elsewhere

Three jailbirds out of six children is going some,
particularly in a relatively law-abiding manor like
Ambridge. **Clive**, Keith and **Susan** (now **Carter**)
have all known the jangle of keys and the slamming
of doors, although to be fair Clive was really to
blame for Susan's incarceration. Their brothers
Stewart and Gary aren't exactly feckful, and Tracy
has exhausted the patience of numerous local
employers, including the **Bridge Farm** dairy and the
café at **Lower Loxley**. Bert is a lengthman by trade
(it's something to do with road building) and Ivy
cleans for **Usha Gupta** at Blossom Hill Cottage. The
phrase 'where did we go wrong?' is a rather over-
used one *chez* Horrobin.

JASON

Borchester
(Brian Miller)

Jason, an ebullient Brummie builder, had three children with his ex-wife, but has lived for many years with his girlfriend in **Borchester**. He's a good craftsman, although prone to taking on too many jobs and so spreading himself thinner than the skim on a partition wall.

JAZZER

Borchester • Born 1984
(Ryan Kelly)

Jack 'Jazzer' McCreary was in **Ed Grundy**'s class at school, and left with a similar lack of qualifications. He originally played drums and later sang in the band *Dross*, with his elder brother Stuart on bass and Ed and **Fallon Rogers** on guitar. But in 2002 his hopes of one day making it onto the front cover of *Kerrang!* magazine were tragically crushed. Always equipped with a dangerously wild streak, he took enthusiastically to a drug called ketamine. After one session with this living death he woke up a week later in hospital. Permanent brain damage has left him clumsy and with memory problems. His shocked friends tried their best to rehabilitate him, but the only contribution he was able to make to the band was as their roadie.

Lower Loxley

What's that stunning bird often seen on the hunt at **Lower Loxley**? No cheap jokes here, please. That's probably a Harris Hawk, in the care of the resident falconer Jessica. She is self-employed, with a *quid pro quo* arrangement whereby she uses premises at Lower Loxley and they are able to offer falconry displays and 'experience days'. She is a good looking woman, though, so it's as well that **Elizabeth Pargetter** is confident that **Nigel**'s interest is purely ornithological.

SATYA KHANNA

ϒ ϒ

Wolverhampton
(Jamilla Massey)

When Usha's family fled from Uganda in the 1970s, they ended up in Wolverhampton, and they really wished that Usha had stayed closer to them rather than moving to **Ambridge**. It falls to Usha's Aunty Satya to act as go-between. She has a knack of sensing when Usha needs a bit of support – or a decent meal cooked from raw ingredients rather than something that involves piercing a plastic lid. Satya always gets on well with **Marjorie Antrobus**, who has seen something of the world and has similar attitudes on many subjects – like the importance of a hot meal on the table.

(Robert Lister)

Life was tricky for **Nigel** and **Elizabeth Pargetter** until Lewis came along. At last; someone who could get the better of indomitable **Julia**, who is remarkably meek in his company. When not on pleasant outings, Lewis and Julia often take charge at **Lower Loxley**'s art gallery, and occasionally look after **Lily and Freddie**. Lewis is an architect, officially retired, but he still does the occasional job that interests him, like the conversion of **Lower Loxley**'s shop and café, the refurbishment of **Arkwright Hall**, or the extension of buildings at The Stables to form **Alistair Lloyd**'s new veterinary surgery.

ALISTAIR LLOYD

The Stables
(Michael Lumsden)

In 2002, Alistair was aghast to find that his partner Theo was stealing drugs from their veterinary practice to fund a cocaine habit. Bruised Alistair dissolved the partnership to set up with a graduate assistant in converted buildings at his home, where wife **Shula** runs a riding school. Alistair's first marriage ended when his wife had an affair, and Shula's fling with Richard Locke meant that she and Alistair might not have made it to the altar themselves. But his love for her and her son **Daniel** won out, and he's been a wonderful father to the boy, whom he adopted in 2000. In his spare time, Alistair keeps wicket for, and captains, the **Ambridge** cricket team.

DANIEL HEBDEN LLOYD

The Stables • Born 14.11.94
(Dominic Davies)

Daniel is fascinated by animals, and you might think that he takes after his father **Alistair**, a vet. But Alistair is actually Daniel's adoptive father. The boy's blood father Mark died never knowing that his and **Shula**'s second IVF attempt had been successful, and the pregnancy gave despairing Shula something to live for. In 1998, a mysterious illness was eventually diagnosed as juvenile arthritis, and Daniel is subject to occasional 'flares' of this debilitating condition. No surprise then, that Shula can sometimes be too indulgent of her miracle child. In 2002 Daniel found it difficult to adjust when returning to school after a bout of the illness, and started to bully other children. It was primarily Alistair who could distance himself sufficiently to manage a return to more acceptable behaviour.

SHULA HEBDEN LLOYD

(formally Hebden, née Archer)
The Stables • Born 8.8.58
(Judy Bennett)

Phil and **Jill Archer**'s elder daughter and **Kenton**'s twin. Shula married **Alistair** in 1998, after an unwise dalliance with the then local GP Richard Locke, which lost Shula the friendship of Richard's partner **Usha Gupta**. It was an uncharacteristic aberration for Shula, a regular churchgoer, bellringer and church-warden. Shula's first husband Mark was killed in a car crash in 1994, never knowing that after years of disappointment and treatment for infertility Shula was finally pregnant with **Daniel**. Shula has always loved horses and after twenty years as a chartered surveyor she took over The Stables – as a home and a business – on the retirement of her aunt **Christine Barford**. It soaked up all her capital and is hard work for limited financial reward, but she doesn't regret the move.

LAWRENCE LOVELL

A rather sad little bed-sit in Felpersham
(Stephen Hancock)

'...my greatest moment was when I was understudying the Red Shadow in a West End production of The Desert Song. *I still remember the thrill when the director told me that Maurice's irritable bowel syndrome had flared up and I was to go on...'*

'...I know from my experience as a model for knitting patterns the importance of the pose. I have often been dubbed a great poseur...'

'...In **Ambridge** *they still talk of the courageous casting of my 1998* Aladdin, *which I might say found gold among dross...'*

'...one's leading ladies do have a tendency to fall for one. It's an occupational hazard. Are you doing anything later, by the way...'

Reporter's notes from a press interview to publicise a production of *Grand Hotel* by the Felpersham Light Opera Society, directed by Lawrence Lovell.

To the casual observer, Lower Loxley oozes the luxury of a grander age. But, as **Elizabeth Pargetter** would testily explain, a 300-year-old building takes more than Handy Andy and a bit of MDF to maintain. So to earn its keep, the Hall hosts conferences and takes sightseers. Elizabeth's husband **Nigel** runs falconry courses and displays with **Jessica**. And the grounds boast a vertiginous tree top walk, rare breeds, and an art gallery. Ancient retainers **Titcombe** and **Mrs Pugsley** have been joined over the years by numerous other employees. **Kathy Perks** runs the shop and the Orangery café, employing the culinary talents of Owen, and the table laying skills of **Emma Carter**, among others. **Hayley Tucker** nannies for the Pargetter twins **Lily and Freddie**, and for Kathy's little boy **Jamie**.

Travelling in Africa
Born 22.6.67

For many years, **Jennifer Aldridge** saw only the occasional card or email from her son, who after graduating in agricultural economics settled in Africa, working on farming development projects. But when in 2001 Adam became godfather to his niece **Noluthando Madikane**, Jennifer and **Brian** were delighted to meet up with him in South Africa. In 1967, Adam's arrival in **Ambridge** caused quite a stir. Jennifer was unmarried and refused to name the father (although Adam's shock of red hair implicated Paddy Redmond, **Phil Archer**'s cowman). Adam was later adopted by Jennifer's first husband Roger Travers-Macy. Eventually the hard life of the development worker took its toll on Adam, who decided he wanted to travel, leaving Jennifer hoping that she might see a little more of him in the future.

KATE MADIKANE

(née Aldridge)
Johannesburg • Born 30.9.77
(Kellie Bright)

Kate's packed a lot into her first quarter-century. In her teenage years she graduated from straightforward mischief to out-and-out rebellion against her wealthy parents, **Brian** and **Jennifer Aldridge**. She took up with travellers and for a while was something of an eco-warrior. She had a daughter **Phoebe Aldridge**, initially fighting **Roy Tucker**'s attempts to prove himself the father. But eventually she had to leave Phoebe with Roy when she travelled to Africa to 'find herself'. In 2001, she returned to **Ambridge** to give birth to her second daughter **Noluthando**, later marrying the child's father **Lucas** in his native South Africa. Kate's occasional visits to her home village are always fraught with tension, because she still feels herself to be Phoebe's mother, even if in reality the role has passed to Roy's wife **Hayley**.

LUCAS MADIKANE

Johannesburg • Born 1972
(Connie M'Gadzah)

The father of **Kate**'s baby **Noluthando** proved his commitment to mother and child when he spent a large sum of money flying to be with them in **Ambridge** after the birth. Caught in the middle of the parental struggle over Kate's other daughter **Phoebe Aldridge**, Lucas eventually managed to achieve the impossible; making Kate see sense. She reluctantly accepted that Phoebe was settled with her father **Roy Tucker** and returned to South Africa, marrying Lucas in June 2001. They are making a success of married life in Johannesburg, where Lucas is a radio journalist with the South African Broadcasting Corporation. They have the occasional (and often slightly fraught) visit to Ambridge, usually funded by Lucas' mother-in-law **Jennifer**.

❡ NOLUTHANDO (NOLLY) MADIKANE ❡

Johannesburg • Born 19.1.01

Lucas and **Kate**'s daughter was born in **Borchester** General Hospital, ironically with Kate's arch rival **Hayley Tucker** in attendance. **Noluthando** means 'one who is loved' in Xhosa, the language of Lucas' tribe. In June 2001 Nolly's grandparents **Jennifer** and **Brian Aldridge** flew to South Africa for the christening, where Kate's half brother **Adam Macy** became Nolly's godfather.

(Anabelle Dowler)

Was Kirsty drawn to **Tom Archer** because of his eco-warrior status, or was the attraction more physical? Either way, Kirsty's own environmental credentials are impeccable, as she too attacked a field of GM crops in 1999. She and Tom were prevented from seeing each other for months while her trial was pending. But once the charges were dropped she reappeared on the scene. Tom was delighted, except for the fact that he had taken up with the more ethereal Lauren Walsh. Tom tried to run both girls simultaneously, but his downfall was just a matter of time. Kirsty eventually forgave him, and enjoys hearing embarrassing stories about Tom's youth from his sister **Helen**, who manages **Ambridge Organics**, where Kirsty now finds a more legal outlet for her environmental enthusiasms.

A farm in name only, this farmhouse with outbuildings and half an acre of gardens is home to **Marjorie Antrobus**. The self-contained flat has been occupied by a variety of **Ambridge**'s young people before their first steps into home ownership, notably **Neil** and **Susan Carter** and **Ruth Archer.** In 2001 it was extended by taking over an existing bedroom to provide a comfy home for **Roy** and **Hayley Tucker** and Roy's daughter **Phoebe**.

ELIZABETH PARGETTER

☙ ☙

(née Archer)
Lower Loxley Hall • Born 21.4.67
(Alison Dowling)

Never afraid to make waves, Elizabeth unleashed a tsunami when she objected to father **Phil**'s plans to pass **Brookfield Farm** on to **David**. (Elizabeth was to receive a mere token; half a £200,000 house.) She protested that running **Lower Loxley** was like knitting submarines out of fifty pound notes, and anyway she was thinking only of **Lily and Freddie**. To be fair, Elizabeth hasn't had it easy in the past. Before her marriage to **Nigel**, she had an abortion after being dumped by swindler Cameron Fraser, and her congenital heart problem required a valve-replacement operation after the birth of the twins. Recruiting **Hayley Tucker** as a nanny, Elizabeth threw herself into keeping the Hall afloat. Despite her spikiness, Nigel owes a lot to his 'Lizzie'.

Lower Loxley Hall • Born 17.8.24
(Mary Wimbush)

Grande dame Julia resents letting *hoi polloi* into her home, even though **Lower Loxley Hall** wouldn't survive without them. Julia would have preferred **Nigel** to marry better than a 'farmer's daughter' (**Elizabeth**), which is ironic as Julia's true past was as a greengrocer's daughter and dancer in wartime variety. Julia has fallen prey to addiction, to alcohol and later to gambling, but in recent years having **Lewis** on hand has helped to curb her excesses, and she's mainly restricted herself to being annoying. Julia was pleased by the arrival of a son and heir in the shape of **Freddie**, seeing **Lily** as rather incidental. But when in 2002 Nigel's sister Camilla and her husband James produced a son – Piers – Julia's delight knew no bounds. At last, a grandchild with breeding on both sides of the family...

LILY AND FREDDIE PARGETTER

Lower Loxley Hall • Born 12.12.99

Elizabeth Pargetter's heart condition would have made even a simple pregnancy daunting, but with twins the pressure was really on. Happily, both were born safely, if early, by caesarean section and soon became troublesome toddlers (what other sort is there?). Freddie (the second and smaller child) used to be the particular favourite of grandmother **Julia**, until **Nigel**'s sister Camilla gave birth to her son Piers in 2002.

Lower Loxley Hall • Born 8.6.59
(Graham Seed)

Nigel and **Shula** (now **Hebden Lloyd**) had some wild scrapes in their youth, he in a gorilla suit and she in a champagne-induced haze. But when Nigel eventually grew up and settled down, it was with Shula's younger sister **Elizabeth**. Often driven as much by his heart as by his head, Nigel became captivated by the sport of falconry, which, thanks to the expertise of **Jessica,** he has made a particular attraction at **Lower Loxley**. Nigel found Elizabeth's wrangling over the inheritance of **Brookfield** rather distasteful. Had she not noticed that she lived in a Jacobean manor with hundreds of acres of parkland and several tenanted farms? Elizabeth countered with the frustrations of propping up a decaying antique, but she might have been talking about Nigel's mother **Julia**.

(née Bone)
The Dower House • Born 3.4.55
(Sara Coward)

Shula Hebden Lloyd's best friend, Caroline is an exquisite bud on the bush of the British aristocracy (related to Lord Netherbourne). She must love her job as manager of **Grey Gables** because she certainly isn't short of a pound for the gas meter. After two decades of doomed relationships (including one with **Brian Aldridge**), a happy marriage to wealthy landowner Guy Pemberton was cut tragically short by his early death. But it left Caroline well provided for, with an annuity, the Dower House and a substantial share of **The Bull**. She eventually found an amiable relationship with another rich man, **Oliver Sterling**. Despite being afflicted with the ghastly burdens of class, wealth, ability, looks and an impeccable riding style, Caroline can still demonstrate the common touch, so necessary when **William Grundy** is your godson and lodger.

April Cottage • Born 20.7.95
(Ben Ratley)

Jamie attends Loxley Barratt Primary and lives with his mother **Kathy**. Ironically, it was Jamie's arrival relatively late in **Sid**'s life which led to his separation from his father. Wanting to keep up with a lively toddler, Sid started a fitness regime. Newly slim, he caught the eye of local siren (that's not a comment on her singing) **Jolene** (now **Perks**), and Sid went from the treadmill to the slippery slope all too quickly. Jamie idolises next door neighbour **Ed Grundy**, whom Kathy has been known to ask to babysit. But only when the remaining population of the Western hemisphere is unavailable.

JOLENE PERKS

(née Rogers)
The Bull
(Buffy Davis)

Jolene's lively personality and generous assets shout 'lock up your husbands' to many Ambridge women, particularly **Clarrie Grundy**, who once saw this singer and keyboard player make beautiful music – well, all right, country and western music – with **Eddie**. But it's **Kathy Perks** who should have been riding shotgun, because she lost her husband **Sid** to the one time 'Lily of Layton Cross' (real name Doreen). Jolene is a natural behind the bar, and much of **The Bull**'s success in recent years has been down to her. She runs line dancing sessions and still has occasional gigs with her band The Midnight Walkers. She's also seen her daughter take the first steps into the music business, although **Fallon**'s preferred style of music is a long way from Nashville.

(formerly Holland)
April Cottage • Born 30.1.53
(Hedli Niklaus)

The 4th July 2002 was a difficult day for Kathy. As her adulterous ex-husband **Sid** got happily hitched to good time gal **Jolene**, it just emphasised the isolation that had already led Kathy (unsuccessfully) into the lonely hearts' dinner party circuit, and to an unwise infatuation with **Kenton Archer**. With experience as a Home Economics teacher and at **The Bull**, at least she is happy managing the café and shop at **Lower Loxley**. Having **Hayley Tucker** as a workplace nanny helps considerably with son **Jamie**, too. Kathy survived the disintegration of her marriage only with the support of her close friend **Pat Archer**. And the **Grundys** next door have their own idiosyncratic approach to neighbourliness, which usually involves finishing Kathy's tea bags and eating all her biscuits.

The Bull • Born 9.6.44
(Alan Devereux)

Despite approaching 60, Sid takes a pride in keeping fit and is manager of the Ambridge cricket team. He has a 49 per cent share of **The Bull** (with **Caroline Pemberton**), a 50 per cent share of **Jamie** (with ex-wife **Kathy**), and a 100 per cent share of **Jolene** (although some **Ambridge** men would love to change that). Sid's first wife Polly died in 1982 and their daughter Lucy now lives in New Zealand. Although usually the classic genial host, on certain topics – like homosexuality – Sid can be pretty reactionary. He clashed with the more liberal Jolene when his step-daughter **Fallon Rogers** started dabbling in drugs, and felt that **Jazzer**'s downfall proved him right. But the disagreement was not enough to scupper Sid and Jolene's spectacular Western-themed wedding in July 2002.

Grey Gables

Lynda Snell has still not forgiven her one-time fellow receptionist at **Grey Gables** for being promoted to assistant manager. On the other hand, what Trudy thinks of young-man-in-a-hurry **Roy Tucker**, whom **Caroline Pemberton** decided to groom for a management position, is not on record.

☠ SOLLY AND HEATHER PRITCHARD ☠

Prudoe, Northumberland
(Solly – James Thackwray
Heather – Joyce Gibbs)

Bluff Solly has the down-to-earth approach you might expect from a man who manufactures toilet paper for a living, and his daughter **Ruth Archer** has inherited a lot of his directness. Heather stands no nonsense either, especially from Solly, but also has compassion in buckets. Although it's a long way to travel, Heather has been a great help at **Brookfield**, both during Ruth's battle with cancer, and after the birth of **Ben**.

CHABA PROGANYI

Brookfield Farm

In the summer of 2002, **David Archer** took stock. **Ruth** was busy with three children, his father **Phil** was retired and **Bert Fry** was getting on. It was clear that **Brookfield** needed some extra help. **Brian Aldridge** suggested he recruit an agricultural student whom Brian knew from his contacts in Hungary. Chaba duly arrived in September 2002, eager to help out and to learn, not just about farming, but about life in Britain too. And quite a few **Ambridge** women were eager to make the acquaintance of this good looking young man, which suited Chaba just fine.

MRS PUGSLEY

Lower Loxley

Of the numerous staff at **Lower Loxley Hall**, housekeeper Mrs Pugsley is one of the longest established. But, like her colleague the redoubtable **Titcombe**, we only ever hear *of* her, never *from* her. Rumours among listeners that the pair of them were installed by the Russians after the unmasking of the Krogers just go to prove that some people should get out more.

Manorfield Close • Born 13.7.15

When people say Manorfield Close is next to Paradise, they aren't praising the facilities but reflecting on the imminent destination of most of the residents. When the last trumpet sounds for the **silent** and weak-bladdered Mr Pullen, he'll probably have to pay one last call before entering those pearly gates.

ELLEN ROGERS

Denia, Costa Blanca.
Born 1926
(Rosemary Leach)

If you heard an infectious laugh drown out the hubbub at **Nigel** and **Elizabeth**'s wedding reception, chances are it came from Ellen (no relation to **Jolene**). **Julia Pargetter**'s sister is a woman who enjoys life, partly because, unlike Julia, she has nothing to hide. She's lived in Spain since her banker husband Harry decided to give up the rat race (well, that was his story) and buy a bar out there. Now she's a widow, the staff run the bar, leaving her time and money to spend as she likes. It's a shame Julia (or Joan, as Ellen insists on calling her) finds Ellen's revelations about their humble past so mortifying, because Ellen is genuinely proud of her sister's success.

The Bull • Born 19.6.85
(Joanna van Kampen)

Although she thinks it's pretty gross, Fallon has more or less come to terms with her mother **Jolene** first having an affair with **Sid Perks**, then moving into **The Bull** and in July 2002 actually marrying him. Following her parents' musical leanings (her father is the country and western guitarist Wayne Tucson), she plays guitar and sings with **Ed Grundy** in the 'metal' band *Dross*. Like her mother, Fallon has an uninhibited streak which males find dangerously attractive. But she tempers it with a degree of steadying common sense. She bolstered her musical ambitions by taking a full-time popular music performance course at **Borchester** College. And while she might smoke the occasional joint, she avoids the chemical excesses which led to the decline of the band's drug-casualty roadie **Jazzer**.

Borchester
(Malcolm McKee)

A land agent working for the **Borchester** firm of Rodway and Watson, Graham was brought in as the hard man to replace **Shula Hebden Lloyd** at the **Berrow Estate** when the then owner Simon Pemberton thought she was being too soft on the tenants. Not that urbane, courteous Graham is a hard man *per se*, but he takes his professional duties very seriously, and he continues to give good service to the current owners, **Borchester Land**. For a while, he courted the lovely **Caroline Pemberton**, even returning to the saddle in an attempt to impress this doughty horsewoman, until to her relief he decided they were better suited as 'just friends'.

ST STEPHEN'S CHURCH

Established 1281

This fine old church dates back to Saxon times. **Shula Hebden Lloyd** and **Bert Fry** (church-wardens), **Neil Carter** (captain of the bell ringers) and **Phil Archer** (organist) have seen some controversy over the years: the installation of a lavatory; clandestine attempts to kill off the bats in the roof; and you don't want to go near the politics of the flower rota. But perhaps the greatest alarms were caused when the parish was merged with three others under the charge of a female vicar, **Janet Fisher**. Although a few parishioners left, most of the congregation eventually adjusted to the changes. But when Janet became entangled in the divorce of **Tim** and **Siobhan Hathaway**, some of the dissenters felt they'd been proved right.

One of the delights of **Ambridge** is that coterie of characters whom the listener knows well and can picture clearly, but who are never actually heard to speak. A large but obviously rather quiet band, they include the ageing **Mrs Potter** and **Mr Pullen** at Manorfield Close, **Lower Loxley**'s talented chef Owen and resident falconer **Jessica**, the quite delectable Mandy Beesborough, the rather less delectable **Baggy**, **Snatch** and **Fat Paul**, **Freda Fry**, exotic east European Anya at **Ambridge Organics**, bellringer Mr Booth, many of the **Horrobins**, and the king of them all, the wonderful **John Higgs**.

LYNDA SNELL

Ambridge Hall • Born 29.5.47
(Carole Boyd)

When Lynda arrived from Sunningdale in 1986 it wasn't long before her name was prefixed by 'oh no, here comes...', because she was determined to bring both culture and green ideals to poor, benighted **Ambridge**. She has embraced numerous fads, often with a New Age tinge, and directed amateur theatricals from panto to Shakespeare (although critics say the two were indistinguishable). When January 2002 brought floods to **Ambridge Hall**, Lynda and **Robert** were touched at the practical support which villagers gave. However, soon the bramble bushes on her way to work (as a receptionist at **Grey Gables**) were once more full of desperate people, diving in to avoid being recruited to her latest project.

Ambridge Hall • Born 5.4.43
(Graham Blockey)

Robert is one in a million; a man who can live with **Lynda** while remaining a. sane, and b. uncharged with murder (or justifiable homicide as it would surely be). A computer boffin with a failed software business behind him, Robert is the calm yin to his wife's incandescent yang. Although actually he'd rather you didn't mention that oriental malarkey, as Lynda's enthusiasm for *feng shui* was one of the more testing things he's had to deal with in recent years. There has often been friction between Lynda and Robert's daughters from his previous marriage, Coriander and Leonie. Although relations with 'Cas' are quite amicable now, Leonie is more obdurate and demanding; usually demanding money, actually. Robert's determination that he *would* help Leonie buy a flat came as quite a shock to Lynda.

OLIVER STERLING

Grange Farm
(Michael Cochrane)

A single man in possession of a good fortune? It is a truth universally acknowledged that Oliver's arrival in **Ambridge** created quite a stir. He sold a large farm in the north of the county to fund his divorce settlement with wife Jane (as amicable as these things can be, he says), and bought **Grange Farm** with 50 acres to do a bit of hobby farming. That work – with occasional help from former Grange Farm resident **Ed Grundy** – left him plenty of time to pursue his passion for hunting, as joint master of the South Borsetshire. Through the hunt, it was inevitable that he would meet staunch horsewoman **Caroline Pemberton**, which soon led to passion of a different sort. Tally ho...

Lower Loxley Hall

Who is that enigmatic figure atop Lower Loxley's mighty ride-on mower? None other than head gardener Titcombe. He's seen a lot of goings-on at the Hall in his time, particularly in the wilder, party-throwing heyday of **Julia Pargetter**. But he never talks about it.

BETTY TUCKER

Willow Farm • Born 4.8.50
(Pamela Craig)

Once a cleaner at **Home Farm**, Betty and husband **Mike** were bemused to find themselves part of the extended **Aldridge** family, as fellow grandparents to **Phoebe**. Energetic and kind hearted, Betty is a staunch WI member, and helps out occasionally behind the bar at **The Bull**. But her main job is managing the **Village Shop** and post office, which provides regular income despite **Mike**'s employment history, which has had as many ups and downs as his emotional state over the years. In 2001, Betty cashed in an insurance policy to contribute towards son **Roy**'s wedding, and decided to start an organic egg enterprise with the balance. Mike went white when she shelled out this nest egg; he thought she was cracked to shoulder this yolk and... (sorry, sorry, I'll stop now).

BRENDA TUCKER

Willow Farm •Born 21.1.81
(Amy Schindler)

Unlike father **Mike**, Brenda rushes at life with naïve enthusiasm. She nearly lost her job as a trainee journalist at Radio Borsetshire when she made allegations on air about corruption involving a local councillor and **Borchester Land**. The story was true, but Brenda had to learn that the law of libel is concerned not with truth but with proof. And she fell keyboard, mouse and monitor for Scott, an actor blown in from the sophisticated warmth of Guernsey. Unfortunately, Scott only saw her as a plaything and was soon off the scene when his sugar mummy **Lilian Bellamy** found he was getting his honey elsewhere. Brenda's appetite for life remains undiminished despite these knocks, but she's a little wiser in the ways of the world.

🌳 **HAYLEY TUCKER** 🌳

(née Jordan)
Nightingale Farm Flat • Born 1977
(Lucy Davis)

Qualified nursery nurse Hayley nannies at **Lower Loxley Hall**. Having bounced into **Ambridge** from Birmingham in 1995, this city girl still can't tell silage from slurry but somehow found that Ambridge suited her and she won the hearts of its inhabitants, with the notable exception of **Helen Archer**. Hayley originally went out with Helen's brother John, but after his death she grew close to John's mate **Roy** and they were married in May 2001. Hayley loves Roy's daughter **Phoebe** as her own but is nervous about her lack of legal relationship with the child. As a result, she is waspishly defensive whenever Phoebe's natural mother **Kate Madikane** is around.

Willow Farm • Born 1.12.49
(Terry Molloy)

In the **Ambridge** Twelve Furlongs Mr Grumpy Handicap Stakes, Mike would finish a nose ahead of **Tony Archer** and a length behind **Joe Grundy**. As a once-bankrupt would-be dairy farmer, who lost an eye in a forestry accident. Mike's been in training for the race all his life. After years of chasing casual farm and forestry work, Mike eventually got a more regular job at a turfing company, which he combines with early starts as a milkman for **Borchester** Dairies. He used to run a pick-your-own strawberry plot with **Neil Carter**, and he hasn't forgiven Neil for first going into a manure business with **Eddie Grundy**, and later starting up an egg enterprise with Mike's wife. 'Et tu, **Betty**?', as Mike might have said if he had read the classics rather than the *Daily Mirror*.

Nightingale Farm Flat • Born 2.2.78
(Ian Pepperell)

In his impressionable youth, Roy fell in briefly with the gang of racist thugs persecuting **Usha Gupta**. Fortunately, he saw the light in time and shopped his 'mates', getting a severe beating as a result. Putting the episode behind him, he buckled down at college, eventually graduating in business studies from **Felpersham** University. Casual work at **Grey Gables** led to training for a management position there, and he seemed set on a promising career. More than once, he has had to fight ex-girlfriend **Kate Madikane** for his rights over their daughter **Phoebe Aldridge**. But once Kate settled in South Africa, he was able to give Phoebe the stability that she needed, in partnership with the far more equable **Hayley**, whom he married in May 2001. And a lovely little family they make, too.

A tied cottage at Home Farm
(Marc Finn)

A former design technology teacher and outdoor activities leader, Greg arrived to look after the expanded **Home Farm/Berrow Estate** shoot in 1998. Widely read, he is a useful member of the pub quiz team, but for a long time his private life was a closed book. Eventually, people discovered that he'd become involved with **Helen Archer**. And even Helen took months before uncovering some big truths about Greg's past life: he was divorced, his two daughters Annette and Sonja living with their mother Michelle in France. Oh, and he'd had a vasectomy. Once it was all out in the open, Greg became a little more relaxed, but there is still tension about his relationship with Michelle, and Helen's mother **Pat** can't help worrying that they haven't heard the full story yet.

UNDERWOODS

Well Street, Borchester

Visit UNDERWOODS for all your shopping needs.

The latest designer names in men's and women's fashions.
Kitchenware that makes cooking a pleasure.
Gifts galore, from perfumery to elegant writing supplies.

Try our renowned Food Hall for the finest fish, those special biscuits or deli delights.

Relax in our self service restaurant with the cup that cheers or the lunch that lifts the spirits.

UNDERWOODS – look no further.

Advertisement in *The Borchester Echo*.

THE VILLAGE SHOP

Ambridge

Ambridge is fortunate in still having a village shop and post office, due in great part to the philanthropy of the owner **Jack Woolley**. **Betty Tucker** manages it, with the part-time help of **Susan Carter**. So for a pint of milk, book of stamps or a video – and especially for the low-down on the latest in Ambridge – you know where to go.

The farmhouse is home to **Mike** and **Betty Tucker**, and their daughter **Brenda**. Like **Nightingale Farm,** Willow Farm's land has long since been bought up by others. **Neil Carter** owns eight acres, on which he runs his outdoor breeding herd of pigs, and, to Mike's irritation (he thinks it will never make money), an organic free range egg enterprise which Neil runs jointly with Betty.

HAZEL WOOLLEY

Last seen in Soho
(Jan Cox)

Adopted daughter of **Jack Woolley** and his first wife, Valerie Trentham. The wayward Hazel seldom visits **Ambridge**, to the great relief of all who work at **Grey Gables** and not a few Ambridge residents. Hazel works in the film business, making (according to doting Jack) 'proper films, for the cinema'. No-one is on record as actually seeing any of them, though. Hazel claimed she was too busy to attend her father's eightieth birthday, but stepmother **Peggy** suspects that when Jack is finally called to that nineteenth hole in the sky, Hazel will be there faster than you can say 'last will and testament'.

126